ISBN: 978-1-7345039-1-3

FOREWORD

"Don't be ashamed to weep; 'tis right to grieve. Tears are only water, and flowers and fruit and trees cannot grow without water." - Brian Jacques, British author (1939-2011)

Quite often, a child's first experience with death and bereavement comes when a beloved pet dies. Whether it's due to the passing of a cat, dog, bird, lizard, or fish, the resulting feelings of a child, including disbelief, confusion and anger, can be profound and have long-lasting impact. Even "replacing" the deceased animal with another pet may not fully assuage a child's pain, if at all.

My motivation for writing "Five Trees for Mina" was to help young readers (and their parents) deal with the loss of a pet – to whatever extent possible. Even as an adult, I found that writing the book was a cathartic and emotional experience that helped ameliorate my own feelings of sadness, loneliness and despair. After all, Mina had been in the family for nearly 20 years at the time we had to regretfully say goodbye.

The days that followed Mina's passing were long and empty. I frequently believed that I had seen or heard her around the house before realizing that my imagination was playing cruel tricks on me. On several occasions, I had to suppress the impulse to feed her during the day. The sight of her empty food and water dishes, a catnip mouse (or two) I discovered weeks after she was gone, and even her travel carrier, moved me to tears. I wondered how a child could possibly cope with similar feelings of loss.

My intent was not to write anything that might be construed as "religious," or "spiritual." Instead, I have left it to the reader to lend their own perspective to the story, at their discretion. But, ultimately, "Five Trees for Mina" is really just about a transference of energy. Though a little cat named Mina is gone as we knew her, she lives on in a very different way. It's unlikely that I'll ever actually see the five trees that were planted to honor her memory, but I nonetheless imagine them growing stronger every day somewhere in Minnesota...and it warms my heart and makes me smile. I hope "Five Trees For Mina" does the same for you and your family.

– Tony Lovitt

- Mina and Shelby

This book is dedicated to my beautiful granddaughter
Jordyn Nicole Carr
With love from Grandpa T

Heartfelt thanks to Dr. Julie Sorenson of Governor
Animal Clinic in San Diego, California for taking care
of Mina for nearly two decades.

Five Trees for Mina

Based on a true story

Written by Tony Lovitt

Illustrated by Izzy Bean

Hi! My name is Shelby and I'm going to tell you a story about a very special cat.

When I was a little girl, more than
anything else, I wanted a kitten for
my very own.

But, I didn't want just any kitten.
I had my heart set on a Persian kitten.

I loved their big, brown eyes and cute
little pushed-in faces.

Luckily, one of my Mom's friends knew a lady who owned and bred Persian cats.

She said the "cat lady" had new litter of six Persian kittens.

One Saturday, my Mom, Dad and I drove to the cat lady's house. When we arrived, the lady was in her front yard.

"Hello!" she said. "Are you here to see the kittens?"

"Yes! Yes!" I said.

The lady took us to a room in the back of
her house.

On a blanket inside a cardboard box was
the mama cat and her six kittens. The
kittens were adorable! So cute and tiny. I
sat next to the box and watched. Then, the
most amazing thing happened.

One of the kittens, a female, stood up and
seemed to walk toward me!

"Mee, mee!" the kitten said in the tiniest voice anyone could imagine.

Was she saying "pick me"? Was she introducing herself? Maybe she was doing both! It was love at first sight, which everyone could see as I played with her.

"I'm going to name her Mina," I said. "It sounds like what she's saying when she talks to me."

Mina was so small, she could have easily fit inside a teacup...with room to spare!

But, for a little kitten, Mina had a big appetite!

Mina ate half a can of cat food, morning and evening, and crunched on dry food in between.

She soon began to expect her meals and learned to answer – in a variety of different voices – three questions I asked before feeding her:

Before I knew it, ten years of fun together -
and hundreds of cans of kitty food -
had passed since Mina had come
home with me.

And I was no longer little.
I was ready to go
off to college.

I couldn't take Mina with me,
but my Mom and Dad took
good care of her.

Mina especially liked to nestle
between my Dad's legs and the
back of the couch as he watched
TV. She felt safe and cozy and
she easily dozed off in that small
space, purring loudly.

Mina loved being lightly
scratched on her head,
behind her ears
and under her chin.

One day, when my Dad touched underneath Mina's chin, he felt a couple of large lumps.

Immediately, he knew something was wrong.

He and my Mom took Mina to the veterinarian the next day.

The vet said Mina had a serious disease called lymphoma…a kind of cancer. Mina's future was uncertain.

Miraculously, even more than two years later, Mina actually seemed mostly the same. The vet declared Mina an "animal medical marvel!"

Nobody thought Mina would still be around to celebrate her 18th birthday (88 in human years), but she was!

But not long after the birthday celebration, Mina wasn't herself.

She had very little appetite and she slept for most of the day. Worse, Mina was regularly getting sick and she often forgot to properly use her kitty box.

My Mom and Dad called to tell me.
After all, Mina was still my cat and I loved her.

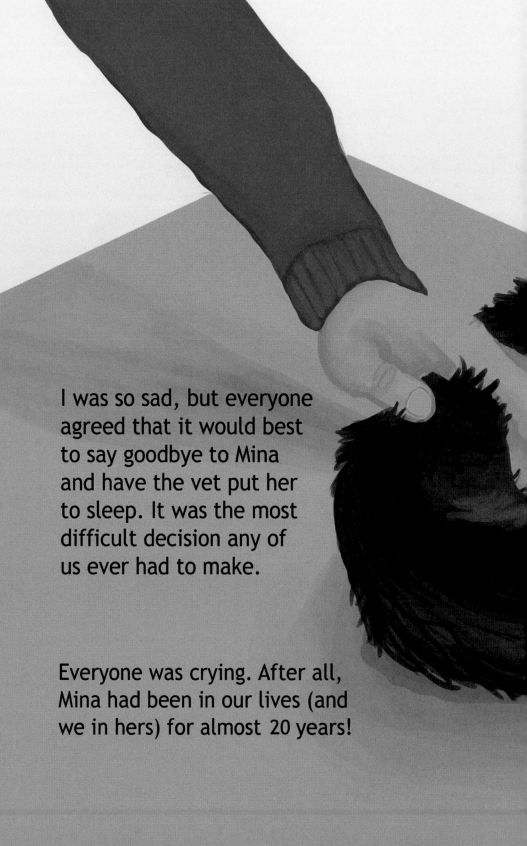

I was so sad, but everyone
agreed that it would best
to say goodbye to Mina
and have the vet put her
to sleep. It was the most
difficult decision any of
us ever had to make.

Everyone was crying. After all,
Mina had been in our lives (and
we in hers) for almost 20 years!

So, my Mom and Dad took Mina
to the vet for the last time.

The days that followed Mina's passing were filled with sadness and emptiness for us all. My Mom and Dad went downstairs, expecting Mina to be waiting for her breakfast, only to realize that she was no longer there.

The "three questions" would no longer be asked or answered.

A few weeks later, a wonderful card arrived in the mail. It read:

*"The Arbor Day Foundation has received a donation in memory of Mina.
As a tribute, five trees will be planted in the Chippewa National Forest.*

The memorial was given by your veterinary clinic.

With thoughts of comfort and peace, the trees will be a living monument to your companion."

Wow! Five trees for Mina.
Five trees to stand strong and tall forever.
What a big honor for a little cat.

We loved and cared for Mina for nearly twenty years and she gave us so much joy and love, too. We will always be happy about taking her into our hearts, where she will always be.

Big smiles have now replaced our sadness when we think of our little friend, especially when we think of her memory living on in a huge forest in Minnesota.

We'll always be grateful
for those five trees for Mina.